MW00899959

# PAPER PILES TO FILES

## A Guide to Eliminating Paper Clutter in Your Home

By Kathryn Warden

I always start out by telling my clients a few important facts to help them begin the process. It is important to realize that you are not the only person in the world that has an issue with piles of paper. If that were the case, I wouldn't have any clients or even a business. Papers are a major part of everyone's life. There are many ways to reduce the amount of paper in your home, but there is no way to completely eliminate it. That is the reason you must create a system that will help you to take control of the paper that does come into your home.

It is also important to remember that the piles of paper did not grow overnight, and it is unrealistic to believe they will disappear that fast either. It is very easy to get frustrated with the increasing piles, and feel the situation is hopeless. This guide will teach you how to eliminate those piles, but the process will take time. A very common mistake I hear from my clients when I first arrive is that they have tried in the past, but became overwhelmed and quit. In this guide, I have broken the project down into smaller steps to avoid this crucial error.

The last point, and most important, is to understand that one system does not work for every single person. Look around any office supply store and you will see millions of options for controlling paper. In this guide I will discuss the most common systems that have proven to be successful for a majority of my clients. I will also share some of the secrets and tips I use with my own clients for reducing the amount of paper that comes into our life every day.

Not only will this guide teach you that anyone can learn how to eliminate those piles of paper and create usable files, but it will also help you learn how to defeat paper clutter in the future.

# *Getting Started*

The first step in eliminating those piles of papers is to find a designated space you can work in, and collect all the supplies you will need for the process. Choose a place that is isolated so you will not be interrupted or distracted when you are working on this project. That means turn off the "Hoarders" TV show, stay away from your computer or updating your status on Facebook, and put your iPhone somewhere you can't hear it. One of the biggest problems my clients encounter is that they are easily distracted. Let's face it- filing paper is not fun for anyone except me. Taking out the above distractions should reduce the chance of you finding something...or anything else to do. Also, preferably find a place close to where you will be filing. After you choose a good space, you will need to find some supplies:

- Manila folders

- Hanging folders (See Lesson #16 <u>Color Coding System</u>)

- Box of black garbage bags

- Post-it Notes for labeling files

- Pens, Black Markers, or my preference- a Labeler

- Recycling Bin

- A Shredder (If you don't have a shredder, designate a white garbage bag for paper that needs to be shredded. We will discuss later how to dispose of your private information.)

**\*\*\* It is crucial to have all your supplies in the designated area before you begin. If you are in the middle of sorting, and you forget something, it is very likely you will take that as an opportunity to find something more interesting to do. I like to recommend that my clients spend about thirty minutes to an hour for each lesson. If you feel like working longer, I would never discourage it. This guideline seems to work for even my most unmotivated clients.**

# Lesson 1

## *The 30 Minute Challenge*

Begin by collecting all the papers you want to sort in your designated area. Grab your garbage bags and your recycling bin to start this first challenge. Your goal for this step is to primarily eliminate the trash first. Paper that is considered trash can often account for up to half of all your paperwork. The reason I start my clients with this step is because when they eliminate the trash first, it gives them a feeling of accomplishment. If you feel as if you have made progress, you will feel more confident to move on with the sorting process.

During this challenge you will be creating only one pile- a "keep" pile. You are only spending thirty minutes on this challenge, so your goal is to quickly go through the piles and eliminate only the papers that are considered trash. If you find yourself debating, simply place the paper in the "keep" pile and continue sorting the papers that are definitely trash.

After thirty minutes is complete, it is important to take the garbage bags out of the room when you leave. If you feel like working longer, by all means keep going. Use this challenge regularly when you feel discouraged or overwhelmed. This lesson will give you a sense of accomplishment when you look around and see how much you have purged. If you feel like you are making progress, you will be more likely to continue the arduous task of sorting your paperwork.

One of the major reasons people ignore their piles of paper is because they become overwhelmed. In this guide, I will break down the process into smaller steps called lessons. This is the key to avoid feeling like it is impossible to get rid of all the paper. In some of these lessons, I will share some secrets I use with my own clients to ensure they will not feel overwhelmed and quit.

# Lesson 2

## *Establishing categories*

Congratulations! You have completed the first step and are well on the way to getting rid of those piles of paper. Now that you have gained the confidence that you can handle this process, you are ready to tackle the piles of papers that you have decided to keep. You will be separating the piles into four categories. Find four containers you can use to keep each pile separate and prevent them from sliding into each other. If you have a large amount of papers, boxes work the best. If you have a small amount of papers, file folders will be the easiest to use. Plastic grocery bags work well for something in between. This is also a great way to keep the piles separated if you need to move them to use your designated space for another purpose. Items you will need for this lesson:

Garbage bags

Recycling bin

Shredder

Black marker

Label one container *To Do*, one container *Reading Material*, one container *Papers to be Filed*, and the last container *Miscellaneous.*

**To Do:** These are the papers that you will need to attend to immediately or within the next twelve months. I place bills in this category since paying them should be on your list of things to do. We will create a system in a future lesson to assure that you will never forget to respond to these papers again!

**Reading Material:** Reading material includes catalogs we purchase items from, magazines, newspapers and reference material we refer to on a regular basis.

**Papers to be Filed:**    These are important papers that you need to save, but are not needed on a frequent basis.  Examples would include taxes, health care information, bank information, etc.

**Miscellaneous:**    These are the papers that do not fit into the other categories, and are often the culprit of paper clutter because they don't have a place.  We will find a place for them in a future lesson.

**\*\*\*\* For this lesson it is crucial that you do not spend a lot of time deciding on which category each paper should be put in.  This is where a majority of my clients become overwhelmed and quit.  If you find yourself debating where to put the paper, just put it into the Miscellaneous pile, and continue sorting.  Many times, as you continue with the process, you will find a place to put the paper.**

As you separate the paper into these four categories, you will likely find papers that are trash but have private information on them and need to be shredded to avoid identity theft.  The goal is to shred these immediately as you sort to avoid wasting time looking at this paper a second time.

The key is to spend at least thirty minutes each day sorting your papers into these four piles.  If you spend less than thirty minutes, you won't accomplish enough and you will feel frustrated. Most likely, you will feel great about how much you are purging and will continue past thirty minutes.  Don't forget to take the garbage out when you leave the room.

# Lesson 3

## *Sorting the To Do Pile*

By sorting through the initial paperwork, you have probably found some papers that have reminded you of things that you need to act on. This is your *To Do* pile. These papers usually consist of bills that need to be paid, papers that require action, invitations, tickets, etc. I will share with you my secret for keeping these papers from getting lost in all your other paperwork. An accordion file. The key to organizing your *To Do* Pile is an accordion file. I have found this to work well with a majority of my clients. It prioritizes you paperwork, as well as keeping it visible so the tasks will not be forgotten. I usually recommend purchasing one in the color red or another bright color so it doesn't get lost on your desk, but that is not mandatory. It is crucial to find one that has at least twelve separate sections. Label each section with a month of the year. As you sort through your papers, determine which are most important by placing them in the current month. This simplifies the goal of creating deadlines to complete your tasks. As you continue this system in the future, place new papers in the file as needed. Remember each month to review the folder and take care of all the tasks for that month. If for some reason, you have not completed the task; move it to the next month to ensure you will not forget about it.

**\*\*\*\* It is imperative that you do not place any other type of paper into this file. If you start placing other types of paper into this file, it will become just another miscellaneous pile and your will ignore it.**

# Lesson 4

## *Bills*

One of the most common requests I hear from my clients when I get called for help with paper management is how to set up a system for taking care of bills. Losing bills is the most common complaint I hear from just about everybody. I will share with you the most efficient systems that seem to work for a majority of my clients.

Most of the time I recommend that my clients sign up for online bill paying. I feel this is the most efficient way to keep track of paying your bills. In fact, most companies prefer that you pay online and will encourage it by making the process easy. Simply go to the company's website and create an account. Each company has a different process for online bill paying, but once you set up the account it is much easier to track each month. Some offer automatic withdrawal directly from your bank account so you don't even have to remember, while others offer email reminders when your bill is due. You will find the options on each company's website. Overall, the advantage is that you will not have to worry about the extra paper clutter that comes in the mail each month.

If you are not interested in this process, the most important thing is to create ONE place to keep your bills. I like to recommend a mail sorter, keeping the bill that is due first in front. Some of my clients have found that inboxes, file folders, or envelopes have worked best for them. The key is to place all the bills in this one area as soon as you receive them in the mail. Refrain from putting the bill on the table or the kitchen counter where it will get lost in all the other paper clutter.

# Lesson 5

## *Sorting the Reading Material*

There are four major types of reading material that can cause clutter in your home.  Catalogs that we purchase items from, magazines, newspapers, and reference material that we need to refer to on a regular basis.  Begin by sorting the reading material into these four categories. If you find you have additional categories of reading material, you may create new categories. I do recommend that you refrain from creating too many categories, which can be overwhelming. If you come across some reading material that doesn't fit into these categories, start to place the items in a Miscellaneous pile to avoid wasting time thinking about it.

****The most important rule to follow when sorting the reading material from this lesson is to refrain from using this time to read anything.  This will only slow down the process, and you will feel as if you haven't made any progress.  If you catch yourself reading something, put the item in the "keep" pile until you are finished with your sorting session.

AFTER completing thirty minutes to an hour session sorting your reading material into these categories, I will then give you permission to take a couple items and actually read them.  However, you must put them directly into your recycling bin and get rid of them!

# Lesson 6

## *Sorting the Catalogs*

You have now separated your reading material into categories. In this lesson we will tackle the catalogs first. Catalogs are defined as any reading material that you purchase items from. I like to start with catalogs because they are the easiest to get rid of. Make sure you have your recycling bin and black marker available for this lesson.

The first step is to realize that almost all catalogs are available online. You will find the most current items available there. Sort through your catalogs to see if there are any you feel you still need to keep, and place the rest in the recycling bin. I like to have my clients mark out their name and address with a black marker to prevent identity theft. Someone trying to steal your identity can easily take your address and initiate a "change-of-address" request, effectively rerouting all your mail (and the additional information within).

If you are not familiar with a computer or you wish to keep a catalog, check the date. Catalogs change monthly with only the top selling items. If you are holding on to older catalogs, it is most likely the items will be unavailable.

If you are holding on to a catalog because you feel that you may want to purchase something in the future from it, rip out the page with the item and the phone number and file it in your file cabinet or pin it to a bulletin board in plain sight. You may also use this system if you just think the store is unique and you may use it in the future. Rip off the front page with the contact information, and file it away.

# Lesson 7

## *Sorting the Magazines*

In this lesson, we are going to be taking control of the magazines. This is one of the most common sources of clutter. People keep magazines with the best intention of reading and enjoying them. The only problem is they continue to collect them, and never find the time to read them. That must stop today. In this lesson, I will teach you the secrets for controlling magazines and how to manage magazines in the future.

****Reminder: If you find yourself reading any articles, place the magazine into the "keep" pile and continue sorting until the end of your session.**

I enjoy reading magazines myself, and I understand that it can be difficult to just throw out a magazine. I will share with you the key to being able to let go of a magazine that has been sitting there for a longtime taking up your precious space. It is important to realistically determine how many magazines you can actually read. The average magazine is printed on a monthly basis. Think very carefully about how long it takes you to read one full magazine. We don't usually have unlimited time to sit down and read one full magazine from cover to cover. Determine how long it takes you personally to read a full magazine. Choose one magazine this week and keep it in a special place so you do not lose track of it. Write today's date on the cover, really big, with a dark black marker. Pay very close attention to how long it actually takes you to read the whole magazine in the next month. Does it take you one day to read the whole magazine? A week? Or do you not touch it the whole month? This will give you a realistic perspective, of on average, how long it takes you personally to read one magazine. After you have tried this test, take a real close look at how many magazines you have. On average, it takes most of my clients a full month to read a magazine in their free time. If you have just twelve magazines, it will take you approximately <u>ONE YEAR</u>

to read those magazines.  Realistically, you have about a year of reading to catch up on, _IF_ you read on a regular basis.  If you have more than twelve; do the math, it could take you _YEARS_ to catch up. Also, check dates.  If the magazine is more than a year old, that means you haven't read it the whole year.  Is it realistic to believe you will find time to read an older magazine before you read the most current one?  As you are looking through your collection of older magazines, and you are finding that you are still having a hard time letting go, remember that you can find almost all older magazine issues at your local library or online.

Any magazines that you wish to purge can be put into the recycling bin, but do remember to cross out your name and address with your black marker to avoid identity theft.

Now, what about all those magazines that you want to keep?  Take another quick look through all the magazines left. Without reading anything, rip out all those articles that caused you to keep the magazine in the first place.  Keep these articles in a 9" x 12" envelope or accordion expanding file folder for reading in the future.  Label your envelope or folder with "To read" and let go of the remaining part of the magazine.  When you have time, look through this folder and enjoy.  If you find that you are not reading the articles in this folder, let them go. Continue to use this same system if you find yourself falling behind-rip out only the articles you intend to read and put them in your "To read" folder.  You can also scan all your articles and keep them in your computer to enjoy when you have the time available.

Some of my clients feel that when they put the article away in a file cabinet or an envelope they will forget about it.  I recommend using a bulletin board or magnetic board to display these articles.  If there are too many articles for a bulletin board, I recommend purchasing a binder with clear page protectors and keeping the articles in there.  Keep the binder on a bookshelf to access whenever needed.

Take a moment to look at the folder, and any remaining magazines. Note that as your folder or piles of magazines increase, the constant demand to read them also increases. A good guideline that I like to give my clients is that when the piles of magazines become more stressful than enjoyable, it is time to let the magazines go.

****Tip for maintaining control over your magazines in the future. Think twice about purchasing any new magazines or renewing any subscriptions until you finish the ones you already have. In fact, I always suggest to my clients to cancel any current subscriptions so they can focus on decreasing the amount of existing magazines they already have. If you just can't bear to cancel a subscription, keep in mind that you can pick the most recent one up at the store if you really want to read it. Always ask yourself if you will realistically have time to read a magazine before you buy a new one; or will it add to the pile of existing unread magazines and just create anxiety? Also, be aware major bookstores offer digital subscriptions to magazines that can be accessed from your computer. This way, you will never receive a paper version that will ultimately pile up on your nightstand again.

A large number of my clients also love to keep magazines for recipe ideas. Create a folder, envelope, or binder for these also. Tear out only the recipes you would like to try, and let go of the rest of the magazine.

Another obstacle that I face with my clients is articles they save to give to someone else. Create a file folder or envelope for this also and label it "To send". Keep this envelope near your address book so it is more likely to actually be sent to the person it is intended for. I like to give my clients a goal of emptying it once a month so the articles remain relevant.

At the end of this session, take the time to read and enjoy some of your magazines….. and then get rid of them!

# Lesson 8

## *Sorting the Newspapers*

This lesson we will concentrate on sorting the newspapers.  Another quick reminder:  Refrain from reading any newspapers until after the sorting session.

I usually have my clients follow the same guidelines that you have learned from sorting your magazines.  Take a moment to think about how much you can realistically read.  Newspapers are generally published on a daily basis.  If you have a pile of seven newspapers, that is about one week worth of reading.  If you have a pile of thirty newspapers that will take you a whole month to read- *IF* you read one whole paper every single day.

Look at the dates, and I like to suggest to my clients to recycle all newspapers that are more than a week old.  I will also remind you that the information from a newspaper becomes outdated quickly, and it is more valuable to read the most current issue.

If you are still nervous to let go of these newspapers, let me remind you that older newspapers can usually be found online or at your local library.  If it makes you feel more comfortable, make a list of all the dates on the newspapers that you would like to keep for reading.  Recycle the newspaper, and then take your list to the local library when you have the time and read all the newspapers you wish.  When you read the newspapers at the library, you are doing it when you have the time instead of just letting the ones you have no time to read pile up.

If you do come across an article at home you think you will enjoy, cut it out and keep it in the file folder with all your magazine articles. You can recycle the rest of the newspaper and enjoy the article at another time.

At the end of this session, take some time to read any articles you have saved and get rid of what you can!

# Lesson 9

## *Sorting the Reference Materials*

Now, to make things a little easier on you, we will continue with sorting something a little less challenging-reference materials. Reference materials are defined as magazines or catalogs that people keep to refer to on a regular basis. If you do not have this type of reading material you can skip this part!

Some examples of reference materials would include:

Craft/Hobby magazines- Scrap bookers are famous for keeping magazines to refer to for ideas

Magazines related to your job-I have a lot of clients that work in the fashion industry and love to keep clothing magazines for reference. Physicians, mental health professionals, writers or even lawyers may keep publications to refer to for updated information.

Magazine files are the best way to keep these publications in order. These amazing products can be found almost anywhere and keep the magazines from falling off the shelf. Approximately seven publications can fit in one magazine file, and they can be bought in any color or pattern to match your décor. Keep these reference materials on a bookshelf for easy access, and make sure you label them for easy identification.

**\*\*\*\* Do keep in mind that many of these resources can be accessed online, in which case you may not need to keep them at all!**

**\*\*\*\* Also important to keep in mind: If you are not using these publications on a regular basis, realize that they are taking up valuable shelf space and you may want to let them go!**

# Lesson 10

## *Creating Labels*

Now that you have mastered control over all the "To Do" papers and all your "Reading Material", we can move onto the rest of the papers that create clutter in your home. In the next couple of lessons, we will address the papers that contribute to the majority of paper clutter in an average person's everyday life. This is the paper that frustrates us. It's the paper that clutters our desks, our kitchen counters, and our dining room tables. It's all those important papers that you can never find when you need them. It is that frustration that brought you here. It is all the papers that need to be filed. I define these papers as the ones that you need to keep, but don't need to access on a regular basis.

The first step to creating a filing system is to understand how to label them. I have been in countless of homes and so many clients tell me they actually have a file cabinet, and while there are papers in it-they never use it nor do they even know what is in it. The key to creating USEABLE files is to appropriately label your files. Most people struggle with deciding what they should label each folder, and find that they never look in the file because they don't even know what the label means. The secret is simple. I tell my clients the key to labeling a file is to stop thinking about it so much. Choose something as simple as possible, and the first thing that comes to mind. For example, if you have a folder with all the maintenance records for your car in it and you label it "Maintenance records for Toyota" and then file it alphabetically under "M"- I guarantee you will never find it again. Why would you look under "maintenance"? Label the file "Car" and file it under "C". Simple.

# Lesson 11

## *Sorting the Paper to be Filed*

Way back in lesson 2, we created a pile of papers to be filed. Again, these papers are defined as papers we need to keep, but not access on a regular basis. In the next couple of lessons we will learn how to create useable files to control these papers, and prevent them from getting lost or creating piles throughout our homes. Items you will need for this session:

File folders

Hanging folders

Black marker or label maker

Post-It Notes or pencil

Shredder

Recycling bin

Garbage bags

Begin sorting through the pile, placing the items in file folders as you sort. I like to suggest using Post-it notes or a pencil at the beginning so you have the flexibility to change a label. Place each file folder into one hanging folder. As you continue to sort, you may find you need to create sub-categories. For example, you may have a checking account and a mutual fund at one bank. Label the hanging folder with the name of the bank, and keep several file folders within the hanging folder labeled with each of the accounts you have at that bank. Another category that I usually divide into subcategories is credit card accounts. Now days, stores love to entice you into opening a credit card account by giving a discount on the items you are purchasing.  A lot of my clients sign up, but then find they don't know what to do with all those cards.

While you may enjoy the discount, if you forget how many store credit cards you have-someone can easily steal your identity and you won't know until it is too late.  Create a label for the hanging folder called "Credit cards", and then create file folders labeled with each store and place them inside the hanging folder. Some people prefer to keep the owner manuals for their kitchen appliances, televisions, computers, etc.  Keep in mind that many of these can be found online, and accessed for free.  If you still decide you would like to keep an owner's manual, label a hanging folder with "Manuals" (or something easy for you to remember) and label each file folder with the specific appliance-such as "Stove" or " DVD player ".  Place each file folder inside the hanging folder.

# Lesson 12

## *How long to keep paperwork*

When sorting through your piles, the question always arises as to what papers we need to keep and how long do we need to keep them.  This is the guide I use with my clients.

Bank statements-  Most banks keep their statements online, so I don't like to recommend keeping them.  If you do receive them in the mail, and you don't wish to keep them, you must shred them.  Some of my clients are uncomfortable with getting rid of them, so I recommend one year at the most.

Credit card statements-  One year. (Unless they are used for tax purposes)

Receipts from deposits, ATM machines, or credit cards-  Save only until the transaction appears on your statement and you have verified the information is accurate.  If you are keeping the receipt because you feel you may have a problem with the item, keep these in one area (such as an envelope) and sort through them EVERY month.   Shred the receipts you do not need. (Unless they are used for tax purposes)  Receipts can get out of hand quickly.  Think very carefully about the reason you feel you need to keep the receipt.  If you feel you may return the item, store the receipt in your wallet to remind you to make a decision about the item.

Stock statements-  Until you sell the stock.  If you receive an annual statement, shred the monthly statements and only keep the annual statements.

Pay stubs-  Keep one year until you receive your W-2's, and then check that the information is correct.

Taxes- The IRS defines the period of time in which you can amend your return or the IRS can assess it for additional tax is actually only three years. If you have failed to report income in the past, the period of time increases to seven years. If you have ever filed a fraudulent return, or did not file a return, they suggest keeping your records indefinitely. I tell my clients to keep their records for seven years, and then check with a tax professional or go to www.irs.gov for more detailed information pertaining to each individual situation.

Home improvements- Keep until you sell the house.

# Lesson 13

## *Safety Deposit Box Papers*

As you sort through your paperwork, you will come across papers that should not be kept in your home in case of a fire or theft. These are papers that you should keep in a safety deposit box. Here are some examples of papers that should be kept in a safety deposit box:

Birth certificates

Marriage license

Passports

Social security cards

Wills

Adoption papers

Life insurance

List of home inventory

Appraisals

Title to your car

Property deeds

Divorce settlements

****Keep a list of all the items you have in your safety deposit box, and store it in a file folder labeled "Safety Deposit Box" in your file cabinet. This way you can refer to the list in the file before making an unnecessary trip to the bank.**

# Lesson 14

## *Children's Artwork*

One of the most common requests I get is for help managing the piles of precious artwork created by children.  One of the hardest types of paper to let go of, I also am guilty of holding on to a lot of priceless artwork.  Not making it any easier, is the fact that they can create so much of it in a single year when they are younger.  While I never advocate getting rid of it, one also needs to set a limit.  Choose a guideline of how many pieces to save per year, and make it a goal to keep only that amount of artwork.  Keep in mind as your sort, how many years you will continue collecting and estimate how much room it will take. Some years you may keep more, and some years you may keep less but the key is to keep as close to your limit as much as possible.  Another important step to managing children's artwork is to sort it on a regular basis.  Especially in the earlier years, if you just ignore this type of paperwork it will get out of control fast.

Keeping those points in mind, I understand that children's artwork is valuable and cannot be replaced, so I do have some great tips for saving those important treasures.

Artwork storage boxes can be found at the Container Store.  I love the ones at the Container Store because they are sturdy and they come in a larger size, some artwork just doesn't fit in the standard size.

Dynamic Frames at **www.dynamicframes.com** is the single most creative invention I have ever seen.  These picture frames display one piece of your child's artwork...but store up to FIFTY pieces in the frame!  It looks just like any average picture frame, and you can store all your child's artwork right on your wall!

Another great option I love to suggest to my clients is **www.preschoolpalettes.com.**   This great company photographs all your child's masterpieces, and preserves them in a hard cover book. It is the perfect solution when storage becomes an issue. The less expensive version would be to use any type of binder with plastic page protectors, and create your own book.

By using the same concept as Preschool Palettes, you could also photograph any oversized or three dimensional works of art and create a compact disk or CD.

Also, don't forget grandparents, friends, or other relatives you could pass the artwork onto which would enjoy your child's masterpieces as well.

# Lesson 15

## *Children's School Papers*

Not only do moms have a hard time keeping their children's artwork under control, but school papers have a way of piling up even faster. The amount of school work, flyers, and information that comes home from school can be overwhelming for any parent. Creating a system solely for this type of paper is crucial for every parent. The first step is to create a routine, set up a time that you can go through the papers and train yourself to be consistent with it. You probably already have a regular time that you tend to glance through it, taking out the crucial papers. Most likely, that is a good indication as to what time will work best for you.

The next step is to find a place to store all this paperwork. The space where all the papers naturally pile up is usually the best space because it indicates where you generally unload the backpack, usually a place in the kitchen or near the front door. After that, you must create a system that will help you to keep track of all that school paperwork. There are many different ways to store school papers, and you will have to see which works best for you. I usually recommend wall files or a desktop file. What is more important is that you divide the papers as they come in to avoid losing anything. These are the most common types of paperwork that usually come home in your child's backpack:

School flyers- These are the flyers that come home from the school that explain activities coming up in the near future, schedules for sports, or general information. If there is an activity coming up that you want to remember to attend, post this on a bulletin board so you can see it and it will remind you. If it doesn't pertain to you, throw it out or recycle it.

School contacts- This usually consists of important phone numbers, directories, or email addresses that you must keep for reference.  Purchase a small desktop file system that has separate file folders, such as an accordion file.  Keep all these contacts together in one file and label it "Contacts"

Completed homework-This is the schoolwork that comes home completed.  You must decide when receiving this type of paper if you want to get rid of it, or if it is something you want to hold on to (such as homework with spectacular scores)  If you decide you want to keep it, place it in your desktop filing system, and label it "Completed Homework".   Keep in mind this is only a temporary storage space for this type of paper.  Make an effort to regularly move this type of paper to a permanent location with the rest of the special school papers that we have sorted. (Usually under "School" for the corresponding child)

Homework to work on- This is usually the type of school paper that moms hold onto to remember to review it with their child on a regular basis.  This includes Information for a test coming up, or perhaps a subject that is difficult for your child which needs to be reviewed regularly.  This should also include any homework that takes more than one day to complete.   You may keep this on a bulletin board, or create a file and label it "Current Homework"

If you have more types of paper than this, add a file folder to your desktop file and create more sections.  If you can regularly file these different types of paperwork in the appropriate files, the only papers that should be left over will be current homework that needs to be taken care of that day.

# Lesson 16

## *Miscellaneous Pile*

At the beginning of this guide, we created four separate piles. Let's not forget about all those papers that ended up in the Miscellaneous pile. I have my clients create a Miscellaneous pile because, when you take a long time debating where a piece of paper goes, it can become frustrating. As I have explained before, you want to avoid this because it can be discouraging. Creating a Miscellaneous pile gives the paper a place for that moment so you can continue with the process. Now that you have completed a working filing system, sorting through those papers should be easy. You have created a system specifically for your paperwork and you probably already have a space for many of those papers. If they do not belong in any of the existing file folders, you have learned the steps for creating a new file. Also, after looking at it a second time, you may realize it is now trash and you don't need to keep it at all.

# Lesson 17

## *Color Coding System*

In some cases, I come across a client who has tried an alphabetical filing system, and it just hasn't worked for them. This is where I like to introduce another filing system that works well for those who struggle with the classic alphabetical system.

At the beginning of this manual, I gave you a list of supplies needed. If you would like to try the color coding system, I have my clients buy colored hanging folders instead of the standard green ones. You will still need the file folders, and all the other supplies listed. Using this system, you will be filing your paperwork in groups instead of alphabetically, and each group will be assigned a color. I have separated the papers into groups below, and have noted the colors I usually use for each group. You may add or subtract a group depending on your individual needs, and it is not mandatory to use the colors that I have suggested.

House (purple) This includes all the papers related to your home. For example: renovations, maintenance information, mortgage information, etc.

Money (green) This includes all the papers that relate to your money. For example: bank statements, credit card statements, stock information, taxes, etc.

Medical (Blue) This pertains to all the paperwork that relates to your health. For example: medical records, lab results, health insurance, medical bills, prescriptions, etc.

Family (Orange) This includes any information related to family members. (Excluding medical or money information) For example: school information, copies of birth certificates, etc. I also include pet records in this group because let's face it- they are considered a member of the family!

# Lesson 18

## *Maintaining control in the future!*

We have now successfully created a place for all those action papers, so you will never lose them again. We have explored different options for filing, and created storage options for all your children's masterpieces. Here are some final tips to keep in mind for the future, so you can maintain all the work you have accomplished.

If you want to keep an inbox for papers that need to be filed, make a commitment to clear it out on a regular basis so papers never pile up again. When the inbox is full, empty it.

Whether you have decided on a red folder, accordion file, or inbox for all your "To do" papers- you must be careful about keeping it ONLY for important "To do" papers. NEVER, NEVER, NEVER mix any other papers with this pile, or it will turn into just another pile and you will ignore it. Remember to make a commitment to sort through these papers frequently to avoid forgetting about the important papers inside.

Make an effort to file on a regular basis. Whether you want to commit to 5 minute per day, 30 minutes per week, or 1 hour per month-you *MUST* make an effort to regularly fit filing into your schedule.

Choose the time of day to sort when you have the most energy. If you are exhausted when you come home from work, don't try to sort your papers then- you are setting yourself up to fail. Don't substitute filing for the time of day you usually like to relax and unwind. Choose the time of day when you are usually the most productive.

To remind yourself to regularly file, find a ritual that you regularly do, and file then. For example, if you have decided to file first thing in the morning, you may choose a ritual such as brushing your teeth or drinking your morning coffee to remind you to file.

If you still have a hard time finding a paper in your file cabinet, it is not because you are disorganized. The system you have created is sufficient; you have just labeled it wrong. Rethink the label- remember simple and the first thing that comes to your mind.

Follow this simple rule for all incoming mail: Decide whether you need to file it, act on it, or throw it out as soon as you touch it. Use baskets, an inbox, or other types of containers to keep papers to file and papers to act on separate. This will immensely cut down the time you need to sort, and prevent you from losing crucial papers. Keep a small trash bin, recycle bin, and mini shredder in the same location you sort through your mail. Dispose of the paperwork you don't need immediately.

Now that I have taught you how to successfully manage all your paperwork, I will give you some of the secret weapons I use to decrease the amount of paper that you receive on a daily basis-cutting down on precious time that you would rather not spend sorting.

**www.catologchoice.com** This is an incredible website. Once you purchase an item from a catalog, you will receive new catalogs from that company on a regular basis for the rest of your life. By signing up for a free account from this website, you may select which catalogs you no longer want to receive. This avoids the time consuming task of calling each company individually and cancelling it.

**www.dmachoice.org** This site gives you information for removing your name and address from receiving unwanted junk mail. Priceless.

**www.optoutprescreen.com** This site gives you the opportunity to cancel all credit card offers you receive in the mail.  I highly recommend this to cut down on the chances of identity theft.

Shredding papers with private information is essential in preventing identity theft. You may not own a shredder, or after completing this process, you may have more than your little shredder can handle.   These are some of the places I recommend to my clients:

Office Depot will shred your paperwork for $.99 per pound.  One pound equals approximately ½" stack of paper

**www.freesecureshredding.com**  This shredding service located in Gaithersburg, Maryland is completely FREE!

**www.fairfaxcounty.gov**  Fairfax County offers FREE shredding events at various locations throughout the year.

**www.shredstationva.com**  Shred Station Express provides shredding services in Alexandria, Virginia.

**www.pcrecycler.net**  Offers monthly shredding events in Chantilly, Virginia

Many local county governments offer FREE shredding events in various locations, check your local government website for information.

I have given you an inside look at how an organizer assists clients with eliminating paper clutter in their home. I have broken the guide down into a step-by-step process to remove the risk of becoming overwhelmed and ignoring the piles. I have shared with you some of the secrets and tips I use with my own clients to teach them how to manage this very common issue of paper clutter. With this guide, EVEN YOU can successfully conquer and maintain control in the future over the paper that regularly comes into our daily lives. Congratulations in defeating those piles of papers, and getting rid of all the stress that accumulates from looking at them!

Feel free to contact me at **info@theartoforder.net** if you run into any obstacles during this process.

The Art of Order, LLC offers onsite support to those that have live in Washington DC, Virginia, or Maryland areas. Our organizers come directly to your home and help you clear the clutter from any space. Please visit our website at **www.theartoforder.net** for details about our services. For those outside the Washington DC metropolitan area, we offer online coaching. Please visit our website for details. Online coaching is an easy, convenient option to help you organize your space. Our consultants assist you in organizing any space with phone calls, digital photos, and email. We help you develop a customized plan with clear and easy steps to follow, and assist you every step of the way to achieve your goal of an organized space.

Made in the USA
San Bernardino, CA
18 January 2018